Who Is a Stranger and What Should I Do?

LINDA WALVOORD GIRARD
pictures by
HELEN COGANCHERRY

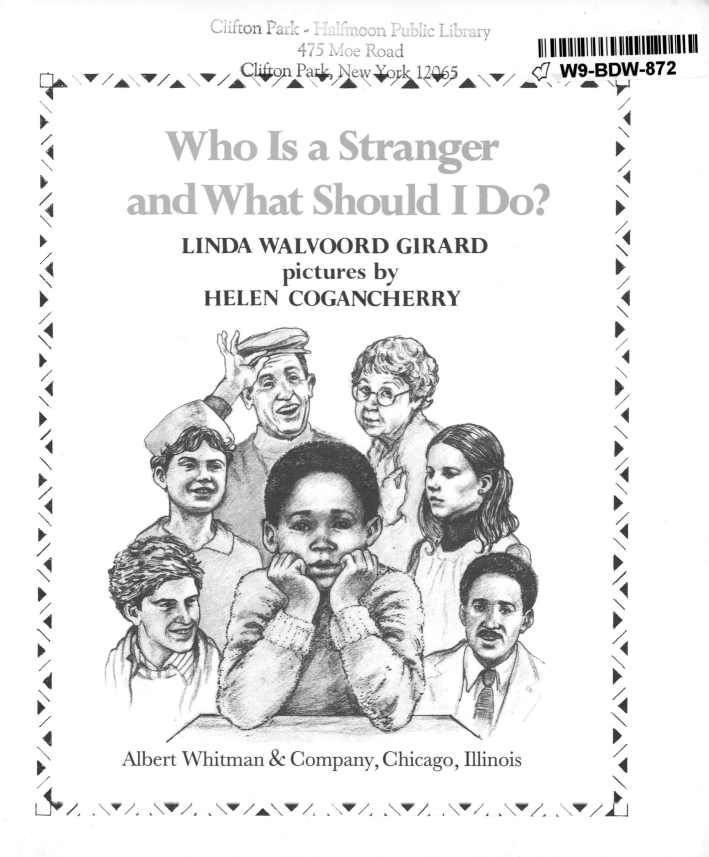

Albert Whitman & Company, Chicago, Illinois

For Aaron. **L.G.**
For Jason. **H.C.**

Library of Congress Cataloging-in-Publication Data

Girard, Linda Walvoord.
    Who is a stranger, and what should I do?

    Summary: Explains how to deal with strangers in public
places, on the telephone, and in cars, emphasizing
situations in which the best thing to do is run away or
talk to another adult.
    1. Children and strangers—Juvenile literature.
[1. Strangers. 2. Safety.] I. Cogancherry, Helen, ill.
II. Title.
HQ784.S8G57   1985   362.7'044   84-17313
ISBN 978-0-8075-9014-0 (hardcover)
ISBN 978-0-8075-9016-4 (paperback)

The text of this book is set in fou tee -point Baskerville.

2818

Contents

E ver since you were a baby, you've met kind strangers. They've talked to you when you went somewhere with a parent or babysitter. Maybe the stranger was a man in the grocery store, a lady at the hairdresser's, or someone on a bus or in the park. "How old are you?" the stranger might have said. "What's your name?" Or "Are those new shoes you have on?"

Your day is more fun when people are cheerful and friendly. Whenever a parent or adult who's taking care of you is right there, it's safe to chat with a stranger.

But you're getting older now. You're out in the world more by yourself. You listen to the news, and you hear your family talk.

You know that once in a great while, there's a stranger who is not a child's friend. Once in a while, a bad stranger wants to hurt a child or take a child away from his or her parents.

The trouble is, that person doesn't always look bad or mean. Bad strangers can be like the wolf Red Riding Hood found in her grandmother's bed. He spoke kind words, but he wanted to hurt her.

Most children will grow up without ever being bothered by a bad stranger. After all, the majority of people are nice. And there are lots of people watching out for you, all the time. Your parents and teachers and police officers and crossing guards watch out for you. It's their job to keep you safe.

But what if a stranger ever does make you frightened or nervous? What should you do? This book will tell you. It's a book for you, about strangers.

Who Is a Stranger?

A stranger is someone you don't know. Even if you recognize people and they act friendly, they're still strangers unless you or your parents know their names and addresses and have gotten to know them well. The garbage man, the grocery-store clerk, and the ice-cream man are all strangers.

A stranger can be a man or woman, young or old. A stranger can wear jeans and a T-shirt or dress up in a suit and tie. No matter how they look, all the people shown on this page are strangers. You and your parents don't know their names and addresses, and nobody in your family is well acquainted with them.

What Should I Do If a Stranger Approaches?

If a stranger passing on the street says, "Hi," it's okay to answer, "Hi." But suppose you're alone or only with other children, and a stranger walks up. He asks you questions about yourself, like "What's your name?" "Where do you live?" "Are you all alone?"

Don't answer! Run! That person might not be your friend.

Suppose a stranger asks you for help. Maybe a lady says she doesn't know the way to Fifth Street and needs someone to walk over there with her.

Don't go! Never go anywhere with a stranger!

It probably feels funny to say no to grownups. You've been taught to be polite and helpful. But you don't have to give help to strangers or answer any questions, especially about yourself.

What if you are pretty sure someone does need help? If you see someone who is injured or looks sick, run and find a grownup. But never go anywhere with a stranger who asks for help!

Ask your parents how you might help someone you don't know.

Strangers in Public Places

Sometimes a bad stranger stands and waits where children play. Of course, most people who stand and wait somewhere are not bad strangers. But here are some things to watch out for.

In school or on the playground: Nobody is allowed to be anywhere in your school or on its playground unless he or she works there, is a parent, or has the school's permission to visit. If you see a stranger in school or waiting near the playground, tell your teacher.

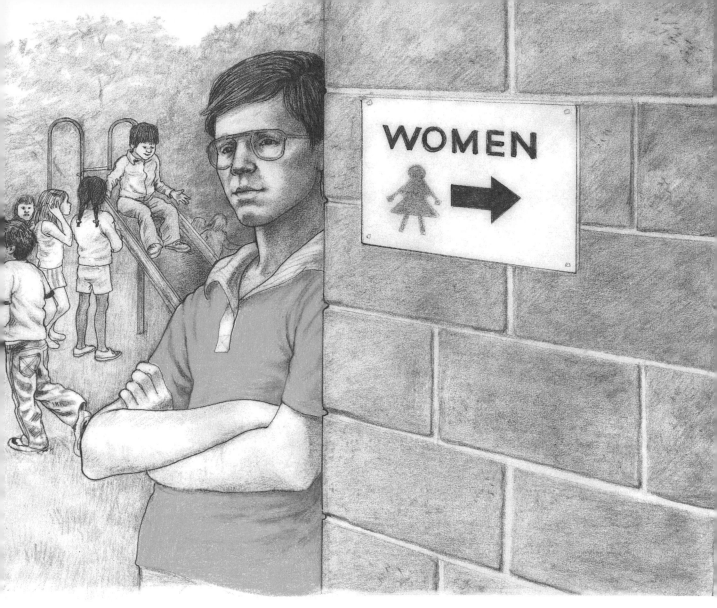

At public bathrooms: When you use a public bathroom (at the movies or in a restaurant), go in with a grownup or another child. Leave as soon as you can; a public bathroom isn't a good place to stay or play. Never go into a bathroom in a deserted place like an empty park.

School bathrooms are okay; they're just for kids to use. But if you see a strange grownup in your school bathroom, leave right away and tell your teacher.

Telephone and Doorbell Strangers

When you happen to be home all alone, someone you don't know may come to the door or call on the telephone. What should you do?

A telephone stranger is someone whose voice or name you don't recognize. Here are some telephone rules:

- Don't give your name or answer any questions until you know who is speaking. Say, "Who's calling, please?"

- Never tell any caller that you are home alone. Ask your parents what you should say if you answer the telephone when they are not at home.

- If you answer the phone and the caller hangs up or says he or she dialed a wrong number, tell your parents.

Here are some doorbell safety rules:

• Before your parents leave, ask them when it's all right to open the door.

• If you expect someone, ask, "Who's there?" before opening the door. Be sure it's the person you're waiting for.

• If a stranger calls out "Special delivery!" or "Florist!" or "Police officer!" don't open the door. You have no way to tell who the person really is. Sometimes a bad stranger will dress up in a uniform.

• Never let a person in just because he or she is wearing a uniform, even if he or she looks like a police officer.

• Ask your parents whether you can speak to a stranger at the door.

• If a stranger keeps ringing, you can call a neighbor or the police to check on it. It's never wrong to ask for help if you're uncertain about a stranger at your door.

The Never, Never Rule

One rule about strangers is more important than any of the others. It's called the Never, Never Rule, and it's very simple.

NEVER, NEVER TAKE A WALK OR GO FOR A RIDE WITH A STRANGER.

If any stranger ever offers to take you somewhere—by car or by foot— yell, "NO!" and run! That person is not acting right. Tell an adult immediately.

If any stranger in a car calls to you or seems to be watching, run away.

Most schools have very strict rules about who can pick you up. These rules say your parents must give permission ahead of time. No stranger should approach you at school or on the way home and say he or she is there to bring you home.

Ask your parents whom they'd let you walk or ride home with. If people you recognize but don't know well offer you rides, explain that your family has rules about whom you can ride with. People will understand. They won't be mad.

Nobody should ever take you *anywhere* unless your parents know about it or have told you that person is all right.

If anyone in a strange car ever asks for help or directions, don't go near that strange car! Usually adults don't ask children for help or directions. They ask other adults.

Presents, Promises, and Lies

Sometimes a bad stranger tries to trick a child by asking for help or offering presents or promises. "Hi," someone might say on the street. "Would you like some free candy?" Or "Would you and your friend like to see a movie?"

Shout, "NO!" and run away!

Another trick a bad stranger might try is to say, "Your mother asked me to pick you up today."

Yell, "NO!" and run!

Or a bad stranger might tell a child, "There's been an accident. Your mother is hurt. Come with me in my car right away."

Say, "NO!" loudly and run as fast as you can! If there's ever an emergency, someone you know will come and tell you. Never believe what a stranger says about an accident or emergency in your family. Ask someone you know to find out if something happened. Never go anywhere with a stranger, no matter what he or she says or promises to do.

Bad strangers sometimes trick children by asking them for help. Suppose a nice-looking lady comes up to you one day and says, "I've lost my spotted dog. Would you drive around the block with me to help me look for him?"

Don't go! Never go anywhere with a stranger!

Anyone who fools a child into going for a ride or a walk can go to jail, just for that, even if the person doesn't hurt the child. The law is very strict because judges and police officers and lawmakers want very much for you to be safe.

Where Can I Run?

If you think a stranger is trying to trick you, yell, "NO!" and run! But don't go off by yourself or try to hide. Keep shouting, and run toward other people. If you're with another child, stay together. Run up to a police officer or a lady with children, or run into a store, restaurant, gas station, or office. If no one's in sight, run up to a house. Tell an adult right away!

Even if it turns out that the person is not a bad stranger, you are right to be careful.

Safety Rules: A Review

You shouldn't be afraid to be out alone or with your friends. Most strangers are really nice people, and they could become your friends if you and your family got to know them better. In fact, all of your friends were strangers to you once! But always remember: strangers don't become your friends just by acting friendly for a few moments. You and your family have to know people well before they become your friends. You must always be careful until you know for sure whether someone can be trusted.

Here are the rules we've talked about that will help you to be careful. Follow them when you're alone or with friends your age.

- Don't answer a stranger's personal questions or requests for help.

- Tell your teacher if a stranger is watching children in school or on the playground.

- Don't use public bathrooms alone. Be sure to leave as soon as you can.

- Don't give information to telephone strangers.

- Don't answer the door unless you know who's there, and your parents have said it's okay.

- Never accept presents from a stranger.

- Do not obey strangers who want to take you somewhere, even if they say they are teachers, police officers, or clergy.

- NEVER, NEVER GO FOR A RIDE OR A WALK WITH A STRANGER.

Things to Ask
My Parents or Teachers

Your parents and teachers can tell you more about when it's okay to talk to a stranger and when it's not. It all depends on where you are, whom you're with, and what the stranger does and says.

Here are some other questions to discuss with your parents:

- Is it ever all right to help a stranger?
- When should I be polite to a stranger?
- Whom can I trust in our neighborhood?
- When I'm away from home, whom can I trust?
- When is it okay not to obey grownups?
- Does our family have any special rules about strangers?

Practice

Read these puzzles about strangers. Talk them over with your parents, teachers, and friends to decide what would be safe in each situation. After you've figured out what you would do, look at the suggestions that follow.

What If...?

1. You go into the boys' bathroom at school. A man is in there. Teachers and other adults who belong at your school have their own bathrooms. This man isn't doing anything wrong; he's just there. What should you do?

2. You're walking the last block home from the school-bus stop. A car slows down, and a man who looks like your grandfather gets out. He says, "Hi" and motions for you to come over. His voice is kind, and he seems to want to ask a question. Is he a stranger? What should you do?

3. You're playing at the park with friends after school. A lady comes up and calls you by name. She says she's from your school. "Your mom called and wants me to give you a ride home right now," the lady tells you. She's smiling, and she looks nice. Is she a stranger? What should you do?

4. You're at the supermarket. Your mom is two aisles away. A woman walks up and says, "Young lady, I'm a candy saleswoman. Today we're giving free candy to all the children in the store. Come out to my car, and you'll get some." Is she a stranger? What should you do?

5. You're standing with your parents at the zoo, watching the bears. A man next to you says, "Did you know these bears like sausages and sauerkraut?" Is he a stranger? Is it all right to talk to him?

6. You and your friend are at a fair, on your way to the ice-cream stand. A young man comes up and says, "Hey, kids! There's a giant, humungous turtle nearby! Want to see it?" He sounds very nice, and he says you'll be right back. Is he a stranger? What should you do?

7. It's summer vacation. While you and your friend are playing on the lawn, the garbageman picks up your family's trash. As he walks by, he says, "What are you two going to do this fine day?" Is he a stranger? Is it all right to answer him?

8. One day you get caught in the rain biking home from the park. A man you recognize from your church drives by in his station wagon. "I'll give you a lift," he says. "We'll put the bike in." Is he a stranger? Should you go with him?

9. You're with a friend in his yard. A police car stops, and an officer gets out. She tells you she has instructions to drive you to the police station. Is she a stranger? What should you do?

10. You answer the telephone while your parents aren't home. A voice says, "Hello, my name is Nancy. I'm with the National Teachers' Association." She starts asking questions about the TV shows you watch. Is she a telephone stranger? What should you say?

Discussion

1. Leave the bathroom right away and tell your teacher.

2. Even though he looks like your grandfather, he is still a stranger. Don't go near him or his car! Don't hide! Yell, "NO!" and cross the street. If you're near home, run there. Otherwise, run toward people.

3. Even though she's smiling and looks nice, she is a stranger, trying to get you to take a ride! Shout, "NO!" and run away. Go toward your friends and, together, run or bike to the nearest house and phone the police or tell adults.

4. Scream, "NO!" and run back to your mother. The lady is a stranger, and she wants you to go to a car! Tell your mom what happened right away.

5. He is a stranger, but it's okay to chat with him. Your parents are right there.

6. Shout, "NO!" and run away toward people. He is a stranger, and he wants you to go for a walk with him! Tell an adult right away.

7. The garbageman is a stranger, but it's all right to answer him. He's passing by, doing his work. But you'd never go anywhere with him.

8. It depends on how well your family knows the man. This is a good puzzle to talk over with your parents. In general, an acquaintance from your church would still be a stranger. You could say, "No thanks. I can't take a ride if my parents don't know about it." He'll understand.

9. Run inside to tell or call someone. Even though she looks like a policewoman, she is still a stranger who wants you to go somewhere with her! A real officer will always ask to talk to your parents. He or she would never take a child away without telling anyone.

10. You don't recognize her voice, so she is a telephone stranger. Don't say your parents aren't home. You could say, "We don't answer surveys by phone," and hang up. Or you could just hang up without speaking. Don't answer any questions or give any information.

Note to Parents

About 1.8 million children are reported missing each year in the United States. Of these, many are runaways or involved in custody disputes. But by various estimates, between 6,000 and 50,000 of the disappearances are due to abduction by strangers. Some of these children never return.

Abduction can happen at any time, in any neighborhood. Children need to learn simple safety rules regarding strangers just as they learn rules for fire and water safety. These rules are best taught through discussion, repetition, and role-playing. Using this book as a starting point, teach a few basic rules so that they become second nature to your children. Discuss hypothetical situations with them. Trust your children's common sense, and encourage them to use it. Tell them that this practice is like a fire drill: most children will never need to use the rules, but they're safer if they know them.

This text stresses that most strangers are nice people. But even a careful, low-key discussion about abduction can leave children uneasy. To reassure your children, remind them that harm from strangers is rare. Emphasize all society does to protect children. When a story about a missing child is featured on TV, point out that it's news *because* abduction seldom happens.

You might also compare familiar dangers. For example, you could say, "You're more likely to break your arm on the playground than to be bothered by a stranger, but you don't spend recess worrying about being hurt." Tell your children that they are safer now that you've talked about what to do if a stranger approaches.

Do make sure that your youngsters know their complete names and addresses (including city and state), how to call the police, and how to phone long distance.

While your children should not become fearful of strangers or withdraw from new experiences, they must understand that abduction can occur anywhere. Show a positive attitude about unknown situations, but stress safety precautions. Alertness and knowledge of safety rules are the best protection your children can have.

Linda Walvoord Girard writes poetry and books for children. She is the author of two other books for Albert Whitman: *You Were Born on Your Very First Birthday* and *My Body Is Private*. Her poetry has appeared in various literary journals. Linda lives in Barrington, Illinois, with her husband and son.

Helen Cogancherry and her husband live in Wallingford, Pennsylvania. They have three children. Helen wanted to be an illustrator from earliest childhood, and drawing is both her profession and her favorite hobby. She has illustrated three other books for Albert Whitman: *Words in Our Hands, Who's Afraid of the Dark?* and *Don't Hurt Me, Mama*.